IMAGES
of America

PALM BEACH GARDENS

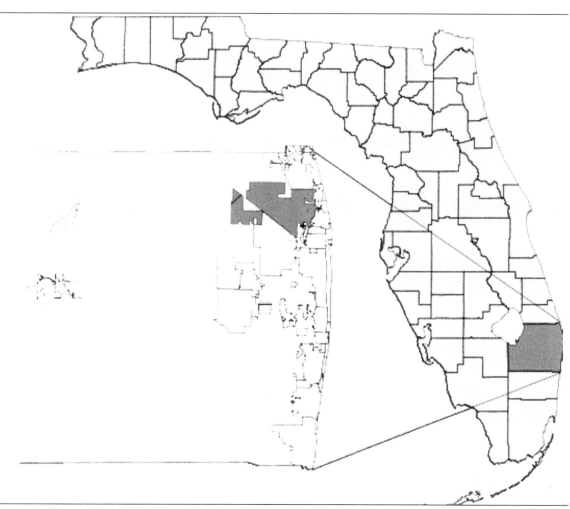

This map of the state of Florida illustrates the location of Palm Beach Gardens, which has a land area of 56.16 square miles. The city, north of West Palm Beach, is in the developed northern part of Palm Beach County and is cut by the Florida Turnpike, Interstate 95, and the Intracoastal Waterway. Palm Beach Gardens, which spreads inland about 25 miles, has at its western boundary the Loxahatchee Slough, a wetland critical to the area's drinking water supply. Palm Beach Gardens is a beautiful, well-planned city, with 30 percent of its land dedicated to green space and many upscale, gated communities. (Courtesy City of Palm Beach Gardens.)

ON THE COVER: In this photograph, taken around 1961, John D. MacArthur (1897–1978), the founder of Palm Beach Gardens, is shown with his dog Zeck in front of the 80-year-old banyan tree he planted at the entrance to the city in 1961. At the city's birth in 1959, the main entrance to Palm Beach Gardens was north of Northlake and Garden (now MacArthur) Boulevards. The banyan tree eventually became the city's symbol. In 2011, the Seminole Chapter of the Daughters of the American Revolution (DAR) succeeded in declaring the banyan tree a Florida Heritage Site. A historical marker was placed by the DAR at the site to commemorate the tree and MacArthur's establishment of the city of Palm Beach Gardens. (Courtesy Palm Beach Gardens Historical Society.)

IMAGES
of America

PALM BEACH GARDENS

Palm Beach Gardens Historical Society

ARCADIA
PUBLISHING

Published by Arcadia Publishing
Charleston, South Carolina

Library of Congress Control Number: 2012938758

For all general information, please contact Arcadia Publishing:
Telephone 843-853-2070
Fax 843-853-0044
E-mail sales@arcadiapublishing.com
For customer service and orders:
Toll-Free 1-888-313-2665

Visit us on the Internet at www.arcadiapublishing.com

The Palm Beach Gardens Historical Society dedicates this book to the past, present, and future residents of the City of Palm Beach Gardens.

CONTENTS

ACKNOWLEDGMENTS

There are many individuals and organizations that provided photographs to the Palm Beach Gardens Historical Society to make this book possible, and we wish to thank them. We also wish to thank the authors, a committee of seven members of the society, who volunteered many hours and searched widely to bring to life the history of Palm Beach Gardens: Suzy Bryant, Arline and Don Kiselewski, Maria Mamlouk, Irene Pedrick, Linda Smith, and Walter Wiley. A special thank you goes to the City of Palm Beach Gardens for allowing us to access their collection of photographs. Unless otherwise noted, all images are courtesy of the Palm Beach Gardens Historical Society.

INTRODUCTION

Carved out of the wilderness of the Everglades, amid pastures and agricultural land, the city of Palm Beach Gardens became the vision of its founder—John D. MacArthur, a wealthy landowner and insurance magnate of Bankers Life and Casualty Company. On March 20, 1959, MacArthur announced his plan to develop approximately 4,000 acres and build homes for a sizeable population in the northern end of Palm Beach County. The City of Palm Beach Gardens was chartered by the State of Florida on June 20, 1959. MacArthur planned a garden city and became personally involved in choosing and transplanting trees from nearby communities and naming streets after flowers and trees.

The early 1960s found MacArthur establishing the foundations of a city: building roads, deeding land for schools, creating public utilities, and beginning the construction of residential housing. MacArthur started selling lots and building homes in the first sections (plats) of Palm Beach Gardens, north of Northlake Boulevard and just beyond Lake Catherine, named for his wife. However, he knew that he needed a corporate infrastructure in order to sell his city's vision. He successfully brought Radio Corporation of America (RCA) to Palm Beach Gardens in 1961, a plant that employed about 2,000 people, and added a recreational draw by luring the Professional Golfers' Association (PGA) of America in 1964. Other major industries that were in the area, where many residents worked, included Pratt & Whitney Aircraft, IT&T, and Solitron Devices.

It was not until 1966 that MacArthur's appointed council gave way to a city council elected by residents. The first council members not appointed by MacArthur were Ted Dela Court and Michael Jackson, who were elected by the residents on April 5, 1965. They were a minority on the five-member council until the next city election in April 1966, when George Bonner, Bill Earle, and Jim Hughes were elected and MacArthur relinquished control of the city. The mayor and vice mayor were MacArthur appointees until Dela Court was named mayor and Jackson vice mayor on April 5, 1965.

As recorded in the 1970 census, Palm Beach Gardens was the nation's fastest-growing city, going from a lone squatter in 1960 to 6,007 residents in 10 years. The 1970s and 1980s brought the development of commercial businesses, including the 1.4-million-square-foot regional shopping center, The Gardens Mall, which opened in 1988.

MacArthur continued his involvement with the city and his extensive landholdings until his death in 1978 at age 80. By then, he was considered one of the two wealthiest men in the country. About $700 million of his fortune was placed into a trust that, upon his death, funded a nonprofit charitable organization: the John D. and Catherine T. MacArthur Foundation. A new wave of growth was created in the city in 1990 when the foundation sold approximately 5,000 acres to developers.

Palm Beach Gardens is a vibrant city with a total 2010 population of 48,452—38.2 percent growth since 2000—and approximately 54,203 during the winter months. It has a land area of 56.093 square miles, of which 30 percent is dedicated to green space. The estimated 2009 median household income was $70,283, and the median resident age was 46 years. The city is an upscale residential community with strict zoning laws and numerous gated communities. PGA Boulevard is the most expensive commercial address in northern Palm Beach County, featuring fashionable shopping malls, office buildings, and a number of restaurants and shops.

The city continues to be the headquarters of the PGA, and there are 17 golf courses within the city limits, including a course owned by the municipality. Several PGA tournaments have taken place in the city, including the PGA Championship, the World Cup, Ryder Cup, PGA Senior Championship, and the Honda Classic. The city ordinance establishing "Art in Public Places" has provided Palm Beach Gardens with a variety of noteworthy public artwork.

In 2009, Palm Beach Gardens celebrated its 50th anniversary, commemorating the occasion with the unveiling of a statue of MacArthur, which was placed at the entrance of city hall. The statue was made possible by a grant from the John D. and Catherine T. MacArthur Foundation. The future economic development of the city has been greatly enhanced with the 2009 arrival of two world-renowned biomedical research institutes in nearby Jupiter: Scripps Florida and the Max Plank Florida Institute.

The *Palm Beach Post*, in a 2005 article on the life of MacArthur, quotes him as saying, "I have always viewed Palm Beach Gardens as something that will live after me, and I am proud of what I have contributed."

One

OUR BEGINNING

Prior to the development of Palm Beach Gardens (PBG) in the 1960s, the area was known for swamplands, cattle ranches, and agricultural land. The first settlers appear to have been residents of Juno, a predecessor of Juno Beach near what is now Oakbrook Square Shopping Center, on the northeast corner of US Highway 1 and PGA Boulevard. Presently, a historic marker is found near the site of the Old Dade County Courthouse (1890–1900).

In the late 1800s, Dade County extended from the Keys to the St. Lucie River, with a population of about 1,000. The county seat had been in Miami since 1844, but in 1889, the North County Pioneers outvoted the South County settlers and moved the county seat to Juno. A two-story wooden structure was built to serve as the courthouse. However, the county seat reverted to Miami in 1900, when Juno lost the election in 1899. Some historians believe a forest fire prior to 1907 destroyed Juno and the courthouse. Others state that the courthouse was moved down to Miami on a barge through the inland waterway and placed on the banks of the Miami River.

Juno was also a transportation terminal for the Celestial Railroad, a 7.5-mile rail connection between Jupiter and Juno. It was established in 1889 to carry passengers and freight, replacing freight wagons pulled by mules. The little railway was in operation until 1896, when Flagler's railroad bypassed Juno.

By the early 1900s, two other areas had been settled: Prairie Siding, a railroad passenger station and site of the Damon timber mill, where RCA Boulevard (formerly Monet Road) meets Alternate A1A; and the embankments of the Intracoastal Waterway, where settlers established prosperous dairy and vegetable farms around what is now Prosperity Farms Road. After 1919, the area was called Kelsey City after Harry Kelsey, a Massachusetts restaurateur who bought 100,000 acres of land, which later became North Palm Beach, Lake Park, and PBG.

In the 1960 US Census, a year after PBG was incorporated by John D. MacArthur, officials found only one inhabitant: Charles Cooper, a 71-year-old man who lived in a shack without water or electricity.

In 1938, unidentified guests of the Seminole Chapter of the Daughters of the American Revolution dedicated the marker of the Old Dade County Courthouse. Juno, predecessor of Juno Beach, was the county seat of what was then Dade County from 1890 to 1900. The courthouse was built on what is today the Oakbrook Square Shopping Center, on the northeast corner of Route 1 and PGA Boulevard. (Courtesy Historical Society of Palm Beach County.)

In 1890, the Old Dade County Courthouse was built at a cost of $1,495. The structure, a two-story wooden frame construction, painted white, housed offices and jail cells on the ground floor and a courtroom on the second floor. The courthouse was the largest assembly structure in Juno and also served as church, lodge hall, and ballroom. (Courtesy Historical Society of Palm Beach County.)

In 1889, the Jupiter and Lake Worth Railroad inaugurated a 7.5-mile line connecting Jupiter and Juno known as the Celestial Railroad. This mid-1890s photograph includes engineer Blus Rice (left, holding the oil can and dog), fireman Milton Messer (polishing headlights), and the conductor, Captain Matheson (on the combination car). (Courtesy Historical Society of Palm Beach County.)

In this mid-1920s photograph, an unidentified Kelsey City resident sports a Panama hat in a sugar cane field in the land named after Harry Kelsey, the founder of Kelsey City—previously Silver Beach—who planned to operate a sugar cane mill. Kelsey, a Massachusetts restauranteur, bought 100,000 acres that later became North Palm Beach, Lake Park, and Palm Beach Gardens. (Courtesy Lake Park Historical Society.)

In the 1920s, early settlements established on the sides of the Intracoastal Waterway became prosperous dairy and vegetable farms and were called Prosperity Farms. Vegetable farms like this bean field grew produce to meet the needs of local grocery stores and hotels. More than 35 varieties of vegetables were cultivated. (Courtesy Lake Park Historical Society.)

The Prosperity Farms Community Council, Kelsey Council Industries, and Kelsey City Brick and Supply Company teamed up to showcase their best vegetables and building products in the 1920s. Here, on February 11, 1924, fresh vegetables are displayed. Two days later, they were sent by train to Madison Square Garden. (Courtesy Lake Park Historical Society.)

The Bonnette Hunt Club Lodge on Hood Road, built in 1968 on leased land, was a private club with some of the best quail hunting, bird dogs, and guides in Florida. The lodge is still in operation today, serving meals and hosting special events. The wildlife hunting grounds later became the golf courses and homes of Mirasol Country Club on PGA Boulevard. (Courtesy Alex Bonnette.)

William A. Bonnette Jr. was a retired Navy warrant officer who developed and ran the Bonnette Hunt Club for over 35 years. When first built, Hood Road was a shell-rock road. Club members used to shoot their quail and enjoy a quail lunch at the lodge. Famous members and guests included King Hussein of Jordan, Bing Crosby, Peter Pulitzer, and many others. (Courtesy Alex Bonnette.)

On October 29, 1970, Betty Alexander of the *Palm Beach Times* reported finding the one inhabitant of PBG identified in the 1960 US Census: Charles Cooper. By then, Cooper was an ailing 81-year-old living in a frame house provided by John D. MacArthur. Above, Cooper (left) is shown talking to MacArthur in 1960. Below, Cooper stands in front of the shack he burned in 1960. MacArthur had made a deal with Cooper, "I told him if he set fire to the old shack I would fix him . . . in a house that would have running water, a toilet, and septic tank to let him live decently." The 1970 Census data showed that PBG grew from one inhabitant in 1960 to 6,007 in 1970, making it the fastest-growing municipality in the nation. (Both, courtesy *Palm Beach Times*.)

Two

The City's Founder, John D. MacArthur

Central to the story of Palm Beach Gardens is the life of its founder, John D. MacArthur (1897–1978). MacArthur, born in a poor area of Pennsylvania, rose from childhood poverty to become a billionaire. By the time he died in 1978 at age 80, MacArthur was believed to be the second wealthiest man in the United States. He made his fortune in insurance, specifically as the sole owner of Chicago-based Bankers Life and Casualty. In the mid-1950s, MacArthur, an eccentric and visionary man, bought several thousand acres in Palm Beach County, creating a real estate empire that comprised land north of Lake Park and south toward Palm Beach. His most ambitious project was the creation of the city of Palm Beach Gardens. In 1959, he applied to the Florida Legislature for the creation of a new city to cover about 4,000 acres, to be named Palm Beach City. However, the State of Florida rejected the name, forcing MacArthur to change it to Palm Beach Gardens. The new name captured and fulfilled his vision of building a "garden city" with roads named for flowers and trees.

In his will, MacArthur assigned $700 million to philanthropy, establishing a foundation named for him and his second wife, Catherine. The John D. and Catherine T. MacArthur Foundation, located in Chicago, is one of the wealthiest foundations in the United States: 2009 data show assets of $5.24 billion and disbursements in that year of close to $300 million in grants and program-related activities to organizations and individuals in the United States and around the world. According to the foundation, "At one time or another, MacArthur's holdings included 100,000 acres of land in Florida, primarily in the Palm Beach and Sarasota areas; several development companies and shopping centers; paper and pulp companies; 19 commercial, office, and apartment buildings in New York City; several publishing enterprises; hotels; radio and television stations; banks; and 12 insurance companies."

John D. MacArthur, seen here with his dog Zeck in the mid-1960s, was born poor, the son of a Scottish preacher in rural Pennsylvania. After dropping out of high school, he became a self-made billionaire. He was eccentric in his personality and lifestyle and was quoted as saying, "Scotsmen are supposed to be very tight . . . I have never denied it. I inherited it." MacArthur called himself "a simple country boy" and lived modestly in a duplex apartment at an old hotel he bought and remodeled, the Colonnades Beach Hotel in Palm Beach Shores. Despite his modesty, his influence in the development of Palm Beach County is second only to Henry Flagler. MacArthur's dog was a Weimaraner named Zeckendorf. He was called "Zeck" for short and was a gift to MacArthur from New York businessman Bill Zeckendorf. (Courtesy City of Palm Beach Gardens.)

The MacArthur family is shown here around 1901 in Scranton, Pennsylvania, before they moved to Chicago. The family first moved to rural northeastern Pennsylvania, then to Scranton, and later to West Pittston. They are, from left to right (first row) Telfer, John, and Charles; (second row) Georgiana, Helen, William, and Alfred; and (standing, right rear) Marguerite. (Courtesy Nyack College Archives and Special Collections.)

The two youngest MacArthur boys, Charles G. (left) and John D., are dressed similarly in this 1904 photograph. Charles, 16 months older than John, went on to become a successful playwright and screenwriter; his second marriage was to the stage and screen actress Helen Hayes. (Courtesy Nyack College Archives and Special Collections.)

Georgiana W. MacArthur poses with John for this mother-son portrait in Chicago in 1909. Georgiana was 40 when John, her youngest, was born. John's parents decided to send their two youngest sons, Charles and John, to a Christian Alliance boarding school in Nyack, New York, and eventually the family followed them, moving to South Nyack. (Courtesy Nyack College Archives and Special Collections.)

MacArthur and his second wife, Catherine T. MacArthur, pose in 1965 with their poodle, Lulu Belle. Catherine became MacArthur's business partner and helped him in his upward climb. MacArthur is reported to have said to his lawyers, when drafting the incorporation papers for the foundation, "Put Catherine's name in there, she helped build it up." (Courtesy Nyack College Archives and Special Collections.)

In 1959, the main entrance to PBG was north of Northlake and Garden (now MacArthur) Boulevards. In 1961, MacArthur transplanted a banyan tree to that site, and the tree became the city's symbol. MacArthur had heard about a resident in Lake Park who was being forced to cut down an old banyan tree, 60 feet high and weighing about 75 tons, and he offered to transfer it to PBG. Unforeseen problems arose during the transplant, including the cutting of the Western Union lines connecting South Florida with the rest of the world. When questioned about moving older trees instead of planting new ones, MacArthur said, "I can buy anything but age. This tree will be the centerpiece of the city's entrance, and while we could plant a little one, I wouldn't be around 80 years from now to see it as it should be."

John D. MacArthur is shown at left in front of the banyan tree he transplanted in 1961. About a year later, a second banyan tree was transplanted. He once said, "I built Palm Beach Gardens without knocking one tree down. There are some bearded jerks and little old ladies who call me a despoiler of the environment. But I believe I have more concern than the average person." Below is the banyan tree in the 1970s.

In the early 1960s, Walt Disney (right) was looking to open a theme park on the East Coast. MacArthur (below) saw this as an opportunity for his new city and proposed land west of the Florida Turnpike, along PGA Boulevard. An agreement was reached. However, the deal fell apart over control of the development surrounding the park. (Below, courtesy Mort Kaye Studios.)

The John D. MacArthur Beach State Park was named after its benefactor, who wanted to preserve the area for future generations, a legacy he left for all Floridians. The park, located on the north end of Singer Island, is a biological treasure. Visitors participate in a variety of recreational activities, including kayaking, bird-watching, fishing, snorkeling, swimming, and boating. Above, at the state park inauguration in 1989, are, from left to right, Larry Martin of the MacArthur Foundation; Mike Martino, mayor of Palm Beach Gardens; John Orr, city manager of Palm Beach Gardens; and Ted Prior of the MacArthur Foundation. Below is an aerial view of the park in the early 1990s.

Three

GOVERNMENT AND PUBLIC SAFETY

Volunteerism, a backbone of American life, cannot be more clearly illustrated than in the early days of government and public safety in Palm Beach Gardens. The city charter, enacted by the State of Florida, provides for a council-manager form of government under which the city council is responsible for the legislative function of the municipality—developing an overall vision, establishing policy, and passing local ordinances and voting appropriations. The city council consists of five residents of Palm Beach Gardens elected to serve unlimited three-year terms. A quorum of three members may conduct city business. The council appoints a professional city manager to oversee administrative operations, implement its policies, and advise it. The mayor presides at all city council meetings, is the head of the city government for ceremonial purposes, and is the city official designated to represent the city in execution of contracts, deeds, and other documents. The mayor is selected by the council from among its members and has a voice and vote in council proceedings. Several advisory committees staffed by volunteers assist the city council with zoning, recreation, beautification, and long range plans. The position of council member was unpaid for many years.

The Palm Beach Gardens Fire Department was chartered on October 9, 1963. Comprised of volunteers, the department operated from a garage, which has since been relocated behind the central fire station at Burns Road and Military Trail. An old pickup truck with 500 feet of fire hose was provided by MacArthur and served the city for several years. The department now operates from five stations with state-of-the-art equipment.

In 1965, the volunteer police reserve force was created. In 1966, Herbert A. Pecht was appointed as the first chief of police. In 1968, three air-conditioned cars patrolled the more than 40 miles of city roadways, and the department was linked to most other South Florida cities by a teletype network system. In March 2000, the police department moved into its present state-of-the art complex. As of 2011, there were 117 sworn and 31 non-sworn staff and 144 various types of vehicles.

Arline Kiselewski, the 1976 Woman's Club president, presented this needlepoint, handcrafted crest to the city as part of the country's bicentennial. It is currently located in the city council chambers. Every member of the club participated in needle-pointing a portion of the crest. Symbolisms of the city crest include the Atlantic Ocean and palm tree–lined beaches; the plaid representing John D. MacArthur's ancestral tartan; the banyan tree marking the first entrance of the city at MacArthur Boulevard; and the family, illustrating the desire to make this city a wonderful place to raise a family. The five stars stand for the five council members who are elected to govern the city.

Meetings of the appointed city council were held in the offices of Bankers Land Company. The first fully elected city council met in Howell Watkins School and later in a rented facility in Meridian Park. After being purchased by the city and renovated in 1968, this old Dr. Pepper bottling plant came to house all municipal offices. Located at the corner of Burns Road and Ironwood Road, today it serves as the Public Works Department headquarters.

This photograph shows the site of city hall from 1971 to 2000. The building was the home of the city manager; the city clerk; and the police, building, recreation, and finance departments until a new municipal complex was completed in 2000, becoming the fifth location of city hall. Also shown are the city tennis courts and the central fire station. A 40,000-square-foot recreation facility was built across Burns Road from the fire station in 1983. (Courtesy City of Palm Beach Gardens.)

A topping-off ceremony for the new municipal complex was held in 1999. Here, signing the last beam are, from left to right, Carl Sabatello, council member; Bobbie Herkovich, city manager; Joseph Russo, mayor; Lauren Furtado, vice mayor; Eric Jablin, council member; and Rex Kirby of Suffolk Construction. (Courtesy City of Palm Beach Gardens.)

Since the printing of the above image showing elected mayors of the city of Palm Beach Gardens, Eric Jablin served as mayor in 2008–2009, followed by Joseph Russo in 2009–2010 and David Levy, who became mayor in March 2010. (Courtesy City of Palm Beach Gardens.)

Appointees to the "developer's council" from 1959 to 1965 included William Cargill, Charles Cunningham, Paul Doolen, James Kelleher, Leo Lehane, Horace Miller, Norman Rowland, and Herbert Thompson (seen here), the first mayor of Palm Beach Gardens.

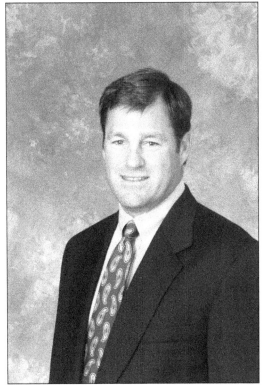

The elected city council members from 1965 to 2011 include Dick Aldred, Jody Barnett, George Blanck, George Bonner, Norman Brown, David Clark, Ted DelaCourt, Annie Marie Delgado, James DeLonga, Robert Diamond, Gordon Dunbar, William Earle, Dick Feeney, Lauren Furtado, James Hughes, Eric Jablin, Michael Jackson, E. Craig James, Henry Jewett, John Kiedis, Don Kiselewski, Samuel Laurie, David J. Levy, Michael Martino, Linda Monroe, John Orr, Bert Premuroso, Thomas Prentiss, Joseph R. Russo, Gerald Rossow, Carl Sabatello, Marcie Tinsley, Hal Valeche, Eugene Walker, and Walter Wiley. David Levy, seen here, was elected mayor in March 2010.

The 1970 city council election was the first time political signs were erected on the side of roadways and in homeowner's yards. Total candidate campaign costs, including the filing fee, were still less than $300 because the hand-painted signs were made with scrap lumber. Council members served without any financial compensation until 1974, when they were paid $50 per month for expenses. Above are, from left to right, James DeLonga, George Bonner, and Greg Bonner. Below are Walter Wiley (left) and George Bonner. Wiley was elected to three consecutive terms and later appointed to a fourth term filling the vacancy of a resigned councilman.

In 1967, the city rented units at 10128 Meridian Way on a temporary lease agreement. The 2,000-square-foot complex accommodated administrative offices and housed the building inspector and the police department. Following a short stay in these facilities, the city offices were moved to the building now housing the Public Works Department at the corner of Burns Road and Ironwood Road.

At the April 4, 1967, organizational meeting, the council unanimously elected Michael E. Jackson as mayor and Robert C. Diamond as vice mayor, and Barney Poston was hired as city manager. Here, George Bonner, City Clerk Thelma Compton, Councilman Gene Walker, Public Works Director Leonard Devine, Councilman Walter Wiley, and Councilman E. Craig James celebrate at a 1970 dinner. (Courtesy City of Palm Beach Gardens.)

The 1970 ground-breaking ceremony for the municipal complex was initiated by Mayor George Blanck, seen here digging the first shovel of dirt. This group of council members includes, from left to right, Councilman Walter Wiley, Vice Mayor James DeLonga, Mayor George Blanck, Councilman E. Craig James, and Councilman Tom Prentiss. (Courtesy City of Palm Beach Gardens.)

The councils of the 1970s concentrated on building the city facilities, authoring the initial code of ordinances, and developing long-range planning for the future growth of the city. Here, the 1971 city council stands with a completed code of ordinances. From left to right, they are Councilman Tom Prentiss, Mayor James DeLonga, Councilman John Orr, Vice Mayor Walter Wiley, and Councilman E. Craig James.

1972

In recognition of his many contributions to the city, John D. MacArthur was as honorary mayor by the 1972 city council. Shown above are, from left to right, Robert Carlson, city manager; E. Craig James and John Orr, council members; James DeLonga, mayor; John D. MacArthur, honorary mayor; Walter Wiley, vice mayor; John Kiedis, councilman; and William Brant, city attorney. Thelma Compton, the city clerk, is seated in front on the right. At right, Mayor James DeLonga presents John D. MacArthur with copy of the proclamation naming him as honorary mayor. (Both, courtesy City of Palm Beach Gardens.)

The 1972 council enacted a building moratorium, stopping all new building within the city due to overloaded sewage treatment facilities. A local court ruled that septic tanks would be permissible in the city until new treatment facilities were available, which took about a year. Shown above are, from left to right, Councilmen John Orr, E. Craig James, and James DeLonga, Mayor Walter Wiley, and Vice Mayor John Kiedis. (Courtesy City of Palm Beach Gardens.)

All council meetings were attended by citizens as well as the city manager, city attorney, and city clerk, who kept minutes of every meeting. Shown here, from left to right, are City Manager George McMahon, Councilmen Walter Wiley and Michael Martino, Mayor John Kiedis, Vice Mayor Gordon Dunbar, Councilman James DeLonga, and Assistant City Attorney George Baldwin. Seated in front is Alice Jean Kerslake, the city clerk. (Courtesy City of Palm Beach Gardens.)

In 1978 and 1979, a group of residents became very active in city politics when the police officers threatened to join the Teamsters Union. The city threatened to abolish the police department and contract with the Palm Beach County Sheriff's Office. One of those residents was Linda Monroe, the first woman elected to serve on the city council. Shown above is the 1980 city council: from left to right, City Manager John Orr, council members Linda Monroe and Dick Aldred, Mayor Richard Feeney, Vice Mayor Samuel Laurie, Councilman John Kiedis, and City Attorney William Brant. City Clerk Linda Ard is seated in front. (Courtesy City of Palm Beach Gardens.)

The first recreation director, Woodrow "Woody" Dukes, was honored at his 1976 retirement party by past mayors. Pictured are, from left to right, John Kiedis, Walter Wiley, Robert Diamond, Dukes, Michael Martino, George Bonner, and James DeLonga.

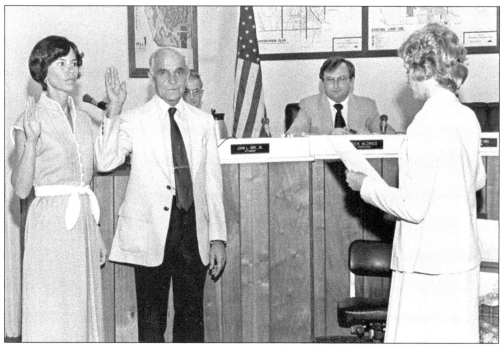

Councilman Dick Aldred looks on as Linda Monroe and John Kiedis are sworn in for the 1980 city council by Linda Ard, the city clerk. Linda Monroe has the distinction of being the only woman to serve as mayor. (Courtesy City of Palm Beach Gardens.)

In the 1980s, the council made a concerted effort to square up boundaries and eliminate unincorporated county land parcels that became enclosed within city boundaries. Here, Don Kiselewski (left) chats with rancher Bill Groot about annexing his 40-acre cattle ranch into the city. Kiselewski was elected to the council in 1981, serving four consecutive three-year terms as councilman, vice mayor, and then mayor.

On July 4, 1972, the city renamed Garden Boulevard MacArthur Boulevard. Right, Mayor Walter Wiley reads the proclamation to John D. MacArthur. Below, the street sign at the intersection of Northlake Boulevard is revealed. In a July 2, 1973, letter to Mayor Wiley, MacArthur stated: "I had no interest in having a street named after me or I would have done so when I named all the streets. I am not a shrinking violet and am proud of the city's skeleton which I built. I think, if the future generations will approve of the original concept and wish to recognize and perpetuate the memory of the founder, I will be proud." (Below, photograph by Katie Diets, courtesy *Palm Beach Times*.)

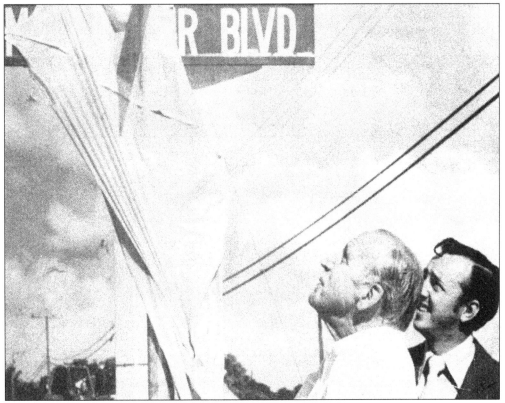

Construction of a new municipal complex was completed in 2000. The police department is in the foreground, the administrative office building on the right, and the central fire station near the top. The old complex, shown in the center of the photograph, was demolished once the employees transitioned to their new offices. During the first 50 years of the city, Barney Poston (1967–1969), Robert Carlson (1970–1972), George McMahon (1972–1973), John Orr (1973–1993), Bobbie Herakovich (1993–2000), and Ron Ferris (2000–present) have served as city managers.

Shown with Santa Claus after the December 1984 council meeting are, from left to right, (first row) City Manager John Orr, City Clerk Linda Ard, and Mayor Mike Martino; (second row) City Attorney William Brant, Councilmen Don Kiselewski and Dick Feeney, Vice Mayor Linda Monroe, and Planning Coordinator Ken Stapleton. Linda Ard was one of only 46 of the almost 400 city clerks in the state to be a certified municipal clerk.

On October 9, 1963, the all-volunteer fire department was formed, initially operating out of an old wood garage at Keating Drive and Northlake Boulevard. That building has been relocated behind the central fire station on the corner of Burns Road and Military Trail and serves as a museum housing the department's historical artifacts. (Courtesy City of Palm Beach Gardens.)

During Fire Prevention Week in October 1978, Fire Chief Ed Arrants dedicated the original fire station "to the memory of the department's charter members, some of whom are still with us, some of whom have passed on, but all of whom have given a great deal to this community." (Courtesy City of Palm Beach Gardens.)

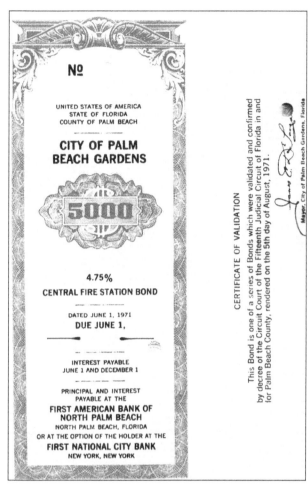

In 1971, voters approved a revenue bond issue (left) to finance the central fire station and to purchase 20 acres of land adjacent to the city property on Military Trail. The 1972 ground-breaking for the new fire station includes, from left to right, Vice Mayor Walter Wiley, Councilman E. Craig James, Fire Department President E.B. Shearin, Fire Chief Millard L. Summers, Mayor James DeLonga, and Councilmen John Kiedis and John Orr. (Both, courtesy City of Palm Beach Gardens.)

Fire Chief Ed Arrants (pictured) served from 1973 to 1998, obtaining the latest in fire protection equipment for the department. He also implemented emergency medical services in the city. In 1998, Arrants was succeeded by Peter Bergel, who began his career with the fire department as an explorer in 1975. At that time, the only paid staff were the fire chief and the fire lieutenant, Bill White. Other fire chiefs were William F. O'Brien (1963–1968), Millard L. Summers (1966–1972), and Antonio P. Morrow (1972–1973).

The city's first ladder truck was a 1941 Peter Pirsch, which served the city from 1977 to 1984. The original fire truck, a 1940 American LaFrance, which served the city from 1964 to 1968, was, Chief Arrants says, "our first for real piece of equipment." It is now housed in the fire museum.

Volunteers are the lifeblood of the fire department, as evidenced by the construction of this training tower in 1979 with contributed labor and materials. Adjacent to the fire museum, this facility contains a smoke chamber, which helps train firefighters under actual fire conditions, as well as a tower for ladder and rope rescue training.

Members of the fire department auxiliary pose beside one of the department's original Ford Atlantic pumpers in the early 1980s. They were wives of the firefighters and participated when called during large fires to provide food and drink for firefighters. They also held fundraising projects and bought equipment and supplies with the proceeds. The auxiliary purchased the Firefighter Memorial, located at Fire Station No. 1. Unfortunately, the auxiliary disbanded around 1999.

Vintage trucks were on display at the 1973 grand opening of the central fire station. In 1987, a condition for approval of The Gardens Mall was for the mall developers to build a fire station at Campus Drive and RCA Boulevard—Fire Station No. 2. These stations were staffed by career and volunteer firefighters. On January 1, 1995, the fire department became the provider of emergency medical services in the city. The department is now a full service agency, offering advanced life support, rescue service, fire suppression, fire safety, and inspection services. It is internationally accredited by the Commission on Fire Accreditation International. As of 2011, the fire department operates out of five fire stations, with 125 personnel providing full fire rescue service, outfitted with state-of-the-art vehicles and equipment strategically located throughout the city to provide exceptional service.

In 1965, the police reserve force was enacted. In 1966, Herbert A. Pecht was appointed as the first chief of police, with a weekly salary of $130. In 1967, the department was housed with city administrative offices and the building inspector in a 2,000-square-foot rented complex. Radar was used to facilitate traffic control, and three sergeants, one detective, nine patrolmen, and four dispatchers carried out the day-to-day functions of the police department. Herbert Pecht served as police chief from September 1, 1966, to October 15, 1976. Other police chiefs have included William T. Edwards (1976–1979), Edward F. Himmelsbach (1980–1985), Harry B. Nolan (1985), Ronald S. Neubauer (1985–1988), Jack C. Frazier (1989–1992), James O. FitzGerald (1992–2003), and Stephen J. Stepp (2003–present).

The 1967–1968 police department includes, from left to right, (first row) John Davis, Capt. Tom Prentiss, Chief Herbert Pecht, and Sgt. Hank Nolan; (second row) Nick Curran, Ron Lick, Howard Fries, Warren Roberts, and Robert Barton.

In 1971, a new two-story municipal complex was constructed to house the police department; city clerk; city manager; the finance, building, and recreation departments; and the city council chambers. In 1974, six air-conditioned cars patrolled the city and the department consisted of three lieutenants, three sergeants, two detectives, fourteen patrolmen, one desk sergeant, and nine dispatchers. Shown above is the 1978 sworn and non-sworn staff.

Chuck Hino rides MC-1, a 1979 Kawasaki, the first police motorcycle. Hino served the city from 1975 to 1993, retiring as a sergeant. As of 2011, the department had seven motorcycles among its 144 total number of vehicles.

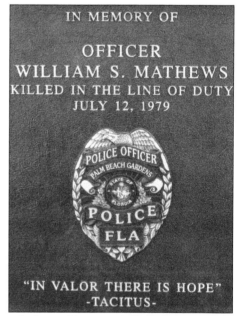

IN MEMORY OF

OFFICER
WILLIAM S. MATHEWS
KILLED IN THE LINE OF DUTY
JULY 12, 1979

"IN VALOR THERE IS HOPE"
-TACITUS-

Officer William S. Mathews, the only officer to die in the line of duty, was killed in a motorcycle accident on July 12, 1979, while attempting to stop a drunk driver. The plaque at right is mounted on a granite base prominently displayed in the garden courtyard outside PBG Police Headquarters.

Staff Photo by Tim O'Hara

Seeking economical performance, the city purchased Chevrolet Nova police cars in September 1975, which doubled the life of the tires while using half as much gasoline as the larger police cars. Lt. Henry "Hank" Nolan stands beside one of the Novas. For one day prior to his retirement, Lieutenant Nolan was honored by being named police chief. (Photograph by *Palm Beach Times* staff photographer Tim O'Hara.)

Officer Robert "Bobby" Wummer (left), with K-9 Kris, and officer Glenn Wright (right), with K-9 Aran, were the city's first canine officers. Officer Wummer has been with the department since April 1984 and with the canine unit since it began in 1994. Wright, now a sergeant, was hired in March 1991. As of 2011, there are four K-9 units in the city.

The SWAT team was formed in 1993 to assist with executing high-risk search warrants, high-risk arrest warrants of dangerous subjects, barricaded suspects, building searches for suspects, hostage situations, or any incident in which there is an elevated danger to the public. Members are highly trained and qualified in the use of special weapons and tactics to fulfill their missions. Two tactical medics are assigned to the team to provide medical support during tactical situations.

The new Emergency Operations and Communication Center, dedicated on June 7, 2011, provides a secure, safe location for the provision of all government and emergency response services. Serving not only Palm Beach Gardens, but also the towns of Jupiter and Juno Beach, this center allows for 72 hours of self-sustained continuous operation during all storm events as well as other hazards.

Four

Early Growth and Development

During the 1960s, the foundations of city government were established, and Palm Beach Gardens began to grow into the "city of the future" with the building of roads, the creation of public utilities, the establishment of schools, and the start of residential housing. The 1970s brought the development of commercial businesses, including the first hotel, the first shopping center, and the first supermarket, as well as the construction of the North County Courthouse complex. The 1980s saw further improvement of roads, additional parks, and the opening of The Gardens Mall, a world-class shopping mall that was the largest in Florida when it was built. The job market continued to grow with city expansion. New industry was attracted to this thriving city and the north campus of Palm Beach Junior College—renamed Palm Beach Community College in 1988 and then Palm Beach State College in 2010—was built to meet the educational needs of a growing community.

The city's first historic district starts at the entrance to MacArthur Boulevard. The great banyan trees that were planted in 1961 and 1962 are in the center oval, framed on both sides of the road with waterfalls flowing over a large rock wall. The rock facade and waterfalls were gone by the 1980s.

New residents of the Gardens often had their family portrait taken at the waterfall and reflecting pond at the entrance to the city, as the Kiselewski family did in 1974. Posing are, from left to right, Arline, Beverly, Don Jr. Karen, Chris, and Don Sr.

The March 1962 Parade of Homes was the second of several annual weeklong events attracting many contractors to the area to showcase their model homes and promote John D. MacArthur's dream of a new "garden city." More than 20 model homes were shown, ranging in price from $15,000 to $25,000. The Parade of Homes events were conducted yearly from 1961 through 1968 and were eagerly anticipated by both the public and builders alike. The 1962 event was attended by over 40,000 visitors, and Palm Beach Gardens was on its way to becoming one of the fastest-growing cities in the country. (Courtesy City of Palm Beach Gardens.)

Bess Myerson, a former Miss America and well-known television personality, participated in the ribbon-cutting ceremony on opening day along with officials from the city and the Home Builders Association. (Courtesy City of Palm Beach Gardens.)

John D. MacArthur poses with Lila Mason, 1962's Mrs. America; 1962's Mrs. Florida; and officials of the city and the Home Builders Association at the opening ceremonies of the 1962 Parade of Homes. MacArthur donated lots valued at over $60,000 for the construction of the model homes. The deeds for these lots were presented to the Home Builders Association, and 20 builders constructed their model homes on these sites. (Courtesy City of Palm Beach Gardens.)

Participating in the ribbon-cutting ceremony for the opening of the 1966 Parade of Homes are, from left to right, Michael Jackson, mayor; Ted DelaCourt, councilman; unidentified; William Storm, president of the Homes Builders Association; Henry "Don" Bogatin, chairman of the 1966 Parade of Homes; John D. MacArthur; and Sy Fine, building contractor.

John D. MacArthur was instrumental in obtaining a Sunshine State Parkway exit into the city of Palm Beach Gardens. He financed the interchange project, and the opening of the exit was dedicated on April 26, 1965. The parkway was renamed the Florida Turnpike in 1968. This interchange was important in providing access to PGA Boulevard and helped to promote residential growth in the western reaches of the city. (Courtesy City of Palm Beach Gardens.)

Dedication Program
April 26, 1965

TURNPIKE

Sunshine State Pkwy

Palm Beach Gardens
Interchange
Sunshine State Parkway

The first two-lane drawbridge spanning the Intracoastal Waterway was completed in 1966 on PGA Boulevard. This bridge was an important link to US Highway 1 from the newly created city of Palm Beach Gardens. The PGA Bridge was also known to locals as the "Please Go Around Bridge" due to its many closings and construction delays during its expansion to four lanes, completed in 1982.

On July 3, 1976, the section of Interstate 95 connecting Palm Beach Gardens with Miami was opened to the public. This section had ended on PGA Boulevard, and it was not until December 19, 1987, that the 44-mile "missing link," from Palm Beach Gardens to Fort Pierce, was finished, finally completing the 1,919-mile expressway running along the entire East Coast from Miami to Maine. (Courtesy City of Palm Beach Gardens.)

Workers assemble personal computers at the RCA plant in Palm Beach Gardens. The city's first commercial building permit was issued in 1960 for the construction of RCA, a manufacturing and electronics company. On May 25, 1961, the $4 million plant opened. It was located at the western end of Monet Road, later renamed RCA Boulevard. The company employed 3,400 people during its heyday, but closed its operations in 1972. (Courtesy State Archives of Florida.)

In 1957, a 7,000-acre tract of swampland west of PGA Boulevard on the Beeline Highway was cleared and drained in what was then part of the Everglades. Pratt & Whitney, an aerospace technology company, was built on this site. Palm Beach Gardens provided homes and a community for many of its employees.

On August 13, 1958, the Beeline Highway was opened to the public. Seminole Indians laid sod and hay on the swale of the newly completed highway. This new east-west extension between Indiantown and West Palm Beach connected Pratt & Whitney with coastal communities and expanded access into Central Florida.

On June 15, 1958, Pratt & Whitney opened on the Beeline Highway west of Palm Beach Gardens. The company developed rocket engines and jet engines that power America's most advanced military fighter aircraft. With nearly 9,000 workers, it was also the largest employer in the county during the late 1980s and early 1990s. The site now houses some of the many divisions of United Technologies Corporation, which have their main offices elsewhere, including Pratt & Whitney, Sikorsky Aircraft, and Pratt & Whitney Rocketdyne.

In 1979, Sikorsky Aircraft moved to the Pratt & Whitney site on the Beeline Highway and began making, improving, and testing helicopters in a building adjacent to the Pratt & Whitney plant. It produced the Army's Black Hawk helicopter and other military and commercial models. Sikorsky has expanded its operations and continues the production and testing of helicopters.

John D. MacArthur (left) shakes hands with contractor Vince Pappalardo at the grand opening of the Tanglewood apartment complex on North Military Trail in September 1971. It was the first apartment rental community in Palm Beach Gardens. The complex was sold in the 1990s and renamed Union Square Apartments. Pappalardo began his career as a building contractor with Fairway Homes Construction Co., building residential housing in northern Palm Beach County. By the 1960s, he had developed a close association with MacArthur and the City of Palm Beach Gardens after designing and building model homes for the first Parade of Homes in 1962 and thereafter. Throughout the 1970s and 1980s, Pappalardo also built many of the city's commercial structures on PGA Boulevard, including the Holiday Inn (now the DoubleTree Hotel), the Radisson Hotel (now the Embassy Suites), and the Admiralty Towers office building. In 1972, Pappalardo completed the Tanglewood shopping plaza, along with the Tanglewood apartments. In 1974, he was the general contractor for the Cathedral of St. Ignatius Loyola. In 1983, he built the city's first community recreation center on Burns Road.

The city's first hotel, a six-story, 126-room Holiday Inn, opened for business in 1970 on PGA Boulevard. It was built by Pappalardo Construction Co. on a seven-acre site close to the PGA headquarters. The hotel served the area's winter visitors as well as the city's many businesses. It also became a social hub for dining and other social events for local residents. The Doubletree Hotel is located on this site today. (Postcard courtesy State Archives of Florida.)

The Admiralty Building, at 4440 PGA Boulevard, was the first multistory office building constructed on PGA Boulevard. Built by the Pappalardo Construction Co., it opened in March 1979. The six-story building cost $2.2 million and had 42,000 square feet of office space. It is at the southeast corner of Military Trail and PGA Boulevard.

Pappalardo Construction Co. was contracted to build the Radisson Suite Hotel in 1987. The hotel opened in 1989, one of five hotels that were either under construction or completed in Palm Beach Gardens during that year. The Radisson Hotel was sold in the spring of 1995 and reopened as an Embassy Suites Hotel. It is located at 4350 PGA Boulevard, across the street from the first hotel Pappalardo built in Palm Beach Gardens.

An unusual feature of the Radisson Hotel was the three mute swans—one black and two white—that lived in the atrium pool in the hotel's lobby. The original swans were brought from Michigan, but currently two male white swans from North Carolina named Bach and Beethoven inhabit the lobby.

Developer Otto "Buz" DiVosta has been an active builder in Palm Beach Gardens for over four decades and has constructed many of the city's homes, townhouses, commercial buildings, and shopping plazas. He pioneered new innovative construction methods, including the development of quick-drying cement, which hastened construction. He also introduced the "assembly line" process of construction allowing him to complete a home in less than 50 days.

Buz DiVosta's first multifamily building began in 1976 with the construction of Sandalwood townhouses. The two-story townhouses featured a four-plex design and used poured concrete construction. This style of home became very popular and offered a well built and affordable home as an alternative to single-family housing. After building thousands of homes and townhouses, as well as many commercial office buildings and shopping plazas throughout Palm Beach County, DiVosta and Company was sold to Pulte Corporation in 1998.

Seymour A. "Sy" Fine established Fine Builders in 1963 and began building residential homes in Palm Beach Gardens. He was one of the first builders of duplexes and multifamily residential and rental units. Fine developed Golfers Village, a one-story duplex development, and built the Heritage Villas on Riverside Drive in MacArthur's first residential neighborhood. He worked closely with John D. MacArthur to develop the core of the city.

In 1963, Fine constructed a two-story office building on the corner of Burns Road and Riverside Drive, the first multistory building on Burns Road. He was an active contractor from the 1960s through the 1980s, and his company continues to manage the residential and commercial properties he built from an office on this site.

The 1978 ground-breaking ceremony launched the start of the PGA National Resort Community. Seen here are, from left to right, J. Richard Ray, vice president of the Manufacturers Hanover Mortgage Corporation; George Hosey, vice president of the Manufacturers Hanover Trust Company; E. Llwyd Ecclestone Jr., developer; Bill Matazenbach, president of Manufacturers Hanover Mortgage Corporation; and John Williams, executive vice president of Manufacturers Hanover Mortgage Corporation. By June 1977, Ecclestone had acquired nearly 2,340 acres of land from John D. MacArthur, with plans to develop it into a residential resort community. The land was just west of the turnpike interchange constructed in 1965. He estimated a $500 million investment would be needed to build his master-planned community. A total of 6,900 homes were scheduled for construction over a 15-year period. The project also included an office park, shopping center, and a light industrial area, as well as golf courses. Manufacturers Hanover Mortgage Corporation of Detroit, Michigan, provided the construction loan of $16 million for the first phase of development for PGA National Resort Community, the new permanent home of The Professional Golfers' Association of America.

Florida's largest shopping mall at the time, The Gardens Mall opened in the fall of 1988 at 3101 PGA Boulevard. This urban center, developed by the Forbes Company, was designated to be the centerpiece for the city's commercial and business district and was carved out of 400 hundred acres of scrub land and palmettos. The mall was originally called The Gardens of The Palm Beaches, but was later shortened to The Gardens Mall. (Courtesy T. Cairns – The Gardens Mall.)

The two-story mall opened on October 5, 1988, and covers 1.4 million square feet of commercial space with more than 150 stores. There were initially three anchor stores—Burdines, Sears, and only the second Macy's in Florida at the time. The mall was the central point of the city's busy retail corridor on PGA Boulevard and a destination point for residents and visitors for shopping and dining.

The Gardens Square Shops shopping plaza was built in 1979 by DiVosta Construction Co. Located at 10900 North Military Trail, on the corner of PGA Boulevard, it is a one-story plaza built on 11.6 acres with more than 5,060 square feet of commercial space. The plaza has several retail stores and restaurants and was the site of the second Publix supermarket built in the city.

Opening on September 4, 1962, Palm Beach Gardens Elementary School was the first of two schools built in the city. It was constructed on 11 acres located at 10060 Riverside Drive and cost $340,000. The school, which opened with 450 students, had 14 classrooms, a library, a cafeteria, a children's room, and staff offices. The original buildings were demolished in 2007, and a new larger school with 48 classrooms opened at the same location in 2008.

Allamanda Elementary School, built on 20 acres at 10300 Allamanda Drive in 1964, was the second public elementary school in the city. The school originally had six buildings: administration offices, a cafeteria, and three classroom buildings with 16 classrooms. In 1975, a media center was added, and in 1987, a 25,000-square-foot expansion added 18 classrooms. In 1990, the school was again expanded to include a new classroom building.

On September 4, 1962, Howell L. Watkins Junior High School opened on Gardens Boulevard (later renamed MacArthur Boulevard). Built on 20.3 acres across the street from the Little League ball field and Lake Catherine, it was the first middle school in Palm Beach Gardens. Edward Eissey was the first principal. In 2005, the original school was demolished and a larger school was built on MacArthur Boulevard and named Howell L. Watkins Middle School.

Palm Beach Gardens High School opened in August 1968 with 1,700 students. It was the first public high school in the area, on Holly Drive just a few blocks from the heart of MacArthur's first neighborhood on MacArthur Boulevard. It was torn down in 2009, and a larger high school was built and named Palm Beach Gardens Community School.

William T. Dwyer High School opened in 1991 at 13601 North Military Trail with 1,161 students. It was the second high school in the city and named for William T. Dwyer, a dynamic civic leader who was the founding president of the Education Foundation of Palm Beach County. It was the fifth high school in the county to offer an International Baccalaureate diploma program.

Edward Eissey, an icon in education, was an educator in Palm Beach County for over 46 years. He was the first principal at both the first junior high school and the first high school. After years as a teacher, principal, and administrator, he became vice president of the north campus of Palm Beach Junior College in 1975, and then president from 1978 to 1997. The campus was named for him in 1990.

The Palm Beach Junior College north campus at 3160 PGA Boulevard was dedicated on June 4, 1982. The college was built on land purchased from John D. MacArthur and opened as a full-time facility, offering associate degrees in arts and sciences and other certificate programs. The name was changed in 1988 to Palm Beach Community College, and in 2010, it was renamed Palm Beach State College.

The Palm Beach Gardens Community Hospital on Burns Road opened on December 4, 1968, and received its first patient, a seven-year-old girl. The hospital cost $1.3 million to build and equip and originally opened as a nonprofit hospital. This 89-bed facility was later given to the City of Palm Beach Gardens by its builder, John D. MacArthur. In December 1970, the hospital was acquired by American Medical International and has expanded several times.

On March 1, 1995, Tenet Healthcare Corporation acquired American Medical International and renamed the hospital Palm Beach Gardens Medical Center. On February 21, 2002, a ground-breaking ceremony for a new $11.2 million addition to the hospital took place. Hospital officials and Mayor Joe Russo (fifth from left) assisted in the ceremony. The expansion included 63 additional beds, a new cardiovascular unit, and a Women's Imaging and Diagnostic Center.

Ground-breaking for the new Palm Beach Gardens Community Center took place in February 1983. From the left are Councilman Michael Martino, City Manager John Orr, Mayor Don Kiselewski, and council members John Kiedis and Linda Monroe. The facility was built on 12 acres and included a municipal swimming pool donated by Buz DiVosta, builder of the "eight-hour house." Pappalardo Construction Co. was awarded the contract for its bid of $1.5 million.

The recreation complex was designed by Oliver and Glidden Architects as a multipurpose facility with a central lobby, a gymnasium, meeting rooms, a performance center, dance and exercise studios, an activity room, an arts and crafts studio, and administrative offices, as well as a community pool. The complex supports the community's recreational needs and serves as a central meeting place for social, recreational, and educational activities.

The Palm Beach Gardens Branch of the Palm Beach County Library opened in November 1977 in an office complex at 10887 North Military Trail. It was the second location for the library, replacing the original site, which opened in May 1975 in the Tanglewood plaza. The library was relocated and expanded over the years before it was permanently moved to a 40,000-square-foot building at 11303 Campus Drive in 2010.

The Northeast Palm Beach County Court House Complex was opened in 1975 at 3188 PGA Boulevard across the street from The Gardens Mall and what later became Palm Beach Junior College. The complex has been updated and expanded over the years and was renamed the North County Courthouse of Palm Beach County.

Five

EARLY HOUSES OF WORSHIP AND SERVICE ORGANIZATIONS

Palm Beach Gardens could be called a "City of Churches," as it counts more than 25 houses of worship within its borders. This is not surprising, as John MacArthur envisioned the city to serve young families fostering strong moral and spiritual values. In fact, according to Nancy Kriplen in *The Eccentric Billionaire*, he asked Billy Graham, who had known MacArthur's preacher father, to establish Billy Graham University in the city. The minister declined, saying he considered himself a preacher, not an educator, and he did not want to spread himself too thin. Disappointed but not discouraged, MacArthur supported the establishment of churches, beginning in 1962. Indeed, after selling land to fledgling congregations, he often contributed generously to their building funds. Service organizations similarly found fertile ground in the Gardens. After the Amara Shriners purchased five acres of land on RCA Boulevard, MacArthur donated an additional five acres.

Donors of heart and hand also were essential to the growth of service and religious organizations. Members of Moose Lodge 2010 saw their home rise, as did the Amara Shriners, as weekend warriors were able to work. Similarly, early churches depended heavily on volunteers to construct their buildings. In addition, when the Trinity Methodist Church moved into its first home, the pastor found himself with an all-volunteer staff.

Christ Fellowship
Gardens North Campus

The Church in the Gardens (Church of God) is the oldest church in the city. In 1962, the West Palm Beach Church of God moved to Palm Beach Gardens and purchased land on the north side of Holly Drive. Until the building was completed later that year, services were held in Rev. L.H. Gillian's Lake Park home. The present sanctuary was dedicated by Rev. Harold Powell in 1976. This church played an important role in the development of Christ Fellowship (left), a church with five campuses in South Florida serving 20,000 congregants each week. Dr. Thomas Mullins and his wife, Donna, as college students in 1967, were summer youth pastors at Church in the Gardens and were befriended by lay leader Richard Smith. He and Rev. Loren Helms counseled the Mullins couple when they decided to leave their business pursuits to found Christ Fellowship in 1984.

The American Lutheran Church Board of American Missions bought five acres on Holly Drive in 1962, and construction of Nativity Lutheran Church began in June. Founding pastor Rev. Dr. David A. Wolber conducted the first formal worship in the completed building on December 23, with 75 congregants. The church officially became a congregation of the American Lutheran Church in 1963 and of the Evangelical Church in America in 1988.

Although Trinity United Methodist Church of Palm Beach Gardens was officially chartered on July 1, 1962, it was not until October 1964 that this chapel was dedicated by Rev. Robert Brittain, and the congregants had a permanent home. The congregation built a fellowship hall in 1966, a children's educational unit in 1970, and a new sanctuary in 1974. The church maintains the nursery-through-fifth-grade Trinity Christian School.

St. Mark's Episcopal Church originated on Advent Sunday in December 1962, when clergy from Holy Trinity Church of West Palm Beach began meeting with a group in the North Palm Beach Elementary School. Under the leadership of Rev. Robert Terhune, the congregation moved to a farmhouse on Alternate A1A and then to its permanent home in 1965. The church founded a prekindergarten-through-eighth-grade school in 1979.

Palm Beach Gardens Church of God, founded by A.T. and Imogene Lowery and Milton and Vonice Pinder, conducted its first service on March 12, 1967, in a private home. In December that year, construction began on a building now known as Carpenter's Chapel. In 1975, the current worship center, seating more than 500 people, was built. It was renamed Cross Community Church in 2010.

When the Gardens Baptist Church at 11980 Alternate A1A was dedicated in May 1962 under the leadership of Rev. Sherman W. Swan, it was not within the boundaries of Palm Beach Gardens. However, with the subsequent annexation of its 3.5 acres, it became the oldest church building in the city. It was renamed the First Baptist Church of Palm Beach Gardens in 1990.

Tropical Sands Christian Church (Disciples of Christ) was organized in 1958 in North Palm Beach, where it remained for 21 years. In 1979, after outgrowing its building, it moved to its new home at 2726 Burns Road, under the direction of Rev. James A. Hilton. With Christian unity as a primary goal, the church actively ministers to community needs. It also operates a preschool.

The Westminster Presbyterian Church, built in 1962 on the corner of Military Trail and Burns Road, is shown here in 1987. In 1995, this church merged with Immanuel Presbyterian Church of Lake Park to form the Gardens Presbyterian Church. The site of the first church is now occupied by the Lakeside Center of the Burns Road Community Recreation Campus. Below, the 1999 ground-breaking ceremony for the new Gardens Presbyterian Church at 4677 Hood Road includes, from left to right, Dr. John Fetzer, pastor Dr. Albert W. Bush Jr., and Samuel Owen. The building was completed in 2001, and the scattering garden in 2002.

The Cathedral of St. Ignatius Loyola began as a parish church designated by Archbishop Coleman F. Carroll of the Archdiocese of Miami on June 25, 1970. The next week, Father John Mulcahy celebrated three masses at the Palm Beach Gardens High School with fewer than two dozen people. With over 600 families by 1974, the church broke ground in January, and on December 14 that year, held mass in the new multipurpose building on Military Trail. On Labor Day 1983, the parishioners laid symbolic stones on the foundation site of their new church. When the Vatican announced the creation of the Diocese of Palm Beach, St. Ignatius Loyola was chosen to serve as the cathedral of the new five-county diocese, with Father Frank Flynn as its first rector. Below, Father Mulcahy breaks ground first in 1974.

Temple Beth David, a conservative synagogue located at 4657 Hood Road, was founded in 1975 in Palm Beach Gardens and moved into its new building in 1983. With about 400 families in its congregation, the temple's sanctuary can be expanded to fit 1,000 people. The temple conducts a preschool and plans a two-story expansion to include a youth lounge and library.

Temple Judea is a Reform Jewish congregation of 550 families whose spiritual leader, Rabbi Joel L. Levine, DD, has been with the organization since its inception in the spring of 1981. Meeting for six years at St. Catherine's Greek Orthodox Church and then on Chillingworth Drive in West Palm Beach, the congregation moved to Hood Road in 2003. Rabbi Yaron Kapitulnik serves as the director of youth education.

This early photograph features two of the first officers of the Kiwanis Club of Palm Beach Gardens, which was founded in early 1983 and officially chartered on April 12, 1984. Shown here, from left to right, are William Bramlett, the first secretary; Jake Swartout; Alexander Ware, the first president; Olin Taylor; and Donald Rachon. An annual football roast is the chief fundraiser for the club's youth activities and scholarships. (Courtesy Kiwanis Club.)

The Loyal Order of the Moose Lodge 2010 was chartered in Lake Park in 1962. However, in 1980, the 1,700-member organization needed more land, and on February 13, 1980, it broke ground on RCA Boulevard to build a new Moose Hall. Besides contributing to Mooseheart, a residential childcare home in Illinois, and Moosehaven, a retirement community in Florida, the lodge sponsors local charitable projects.

Garden Lodge 366 of Free and Accepted Masons was formed in 1968. John D. MacArthur allowed the Masons to meet first in a building on Lake Catherine, before the group moved to the JDM Country Club. Later, the lodge moved into its own home on Roan Lane. The 176 members, under Master Edward Elgin, funnel their charity mainly to the Salvation Army.

The Amara Shrine was organized in Lake Worth in 1974, but it did not have a permanent home until December 30, 1976, when Noble Mathias Jameson arranged the purchase of five acres on RCA Boulevard from John D. MacArthur for $120,000. The center was dedicated on December 10, 1980. The Shriners organization supports 22 Shriners Hospitals for children across the nation.

Six

ORGANIZATIONS, ACTIVITIES, AND EVENTS

Many cities start and grow from scratch but few have achieved as much as the "Gardens." Many cities incorporate and look to their governmental leaders for the impetus to make their city great, supplying all needs by spending taxpayers' money.

There is one thing that has truly set Palm Beach Gardens apart, something that cannot be bought or directed by government. Simply, it is the personal involvement of the residents and their never-ending passion for volunteerism.

Volunteers have made this city great!

Early on, a group of women saw the need to do something special for the youth of the city, so the woman's club was formed. Men likewise started the volunteer fire department and the PBGYAA (Youth Athletic Association). The list of the various individuals and organizations that have contributed to the mix goes on and on. The following is just a small sample of the numerous people and activities that got this city off the ground and flying high.

The Palm Beach Gardens Woman's Club was incorporated and federated in 1967. It is the oldest volunteer organization in the city and has initiated numerous programs and events to enhance the lives of the city's residents. The group's first leaders include, from left to right, Inge Bowdre, Natalie Snyder, Barbara Bruce, president Josephine Saad, Mrs. Bruce Weller, and Thurza Branstrom.

Bingo players celebrate the Fourth of July in a circus tent on Burns Road, now the site of the recreation center, in 1974. One could play for a dime per card or three cards for a quarter, with some prizes reaching $5. While adults enjoyed bingo, children competed in sack races, climbed a greased pole, searched for peanuts, or got cooled off by a fire hose. Many events were sponsored by the Woman's Club.

The city's annual tree-planting ceremony, on National Arbor Day, is sponsored by the Palm Beach Gardens Woman's Club and has taken place in the Woman's Club Honor Park at the south end of Lake Catherine Park since 2001. Prior to 2001, the club planted numerous trees throughout the city.

In 1994, the 12th annual Tasting Tea of the Palm Beach Gardens Woman's Club served over 150 guests. A different theme is chosen yearly, and the refreshments served at the tea coincide with the theme. The event is the major fundraising effort for the club, with proceeds funding the scholarships and other worthy causes for city residents.

"On a Clear Day" was the theme of the unique musical fashion show sponsored by the Woman's Club on November 25, 1969. Members were outfitted as space visitors to advertise the event, and proceeds from the show benefited the volunteer fire department and other community projects. Shown here, from left to right, are Ann Sills, Ann Foster, Pat Bryant, Janice McKaye, and Judy Hood.

This seven-foot sailfish did not get away from Don Kiselewski (left) and his father, Leo, as they fished just offshore from Palm Beach Gardens in 1971. More amazing than its size is that it was caught from a drift boat by two first-time ocean fishermen.

Tots search through hay mounds looking for elusive real peanuts at the Woman's Club event of the city's annual Fourth of July celebration, held on the site of the current recreation building in 1986. This paramount event, for children five and under, continues to this day, although today's peanuts are tiny plastic animals.

Eager to start the annual Easter egg hunt in 1967, these children have come prepared with their various containers to gather up multicolored real eggs. The hunt took place in the vacant land on Burns Road before the firehouse, ball fields, and recreation buildings were constructed.

These young ladies participate in the Junior Miss Palm Beach Gardens contest in 1982. Mayor Don Kiselewski, seated on the lower right, was the "one lucky guy" who judged the contest. To identify participants, each little lady had a banner with her number. The event was held in the PBG High School auditorium.

From left to right, Mayor James Delonga, Tori Keating, Miss Palm Beach Gardens Angel Brazil, Debbie McKinney, and Vice Mayor Walter Wiley pose at the 1970 Miss Palm Beach Gardens Pageant.

The award-winning Palm Beach Gardens High School Gator Band leads the way up Park Avenue, through Lake Park, in the annual Christmas in Dixie Parade in 1976. Under the leadership of its director, Stuart Brenner, the band consistently earned "superior" ratings in both marching and concert competitions.

The 1982 Palm Beach Gardens High School Flag Corps includes, from left to right, Debbie Scarbro, April Swain, Dianne Johnson, Beverly Kiselewski (captain), Jennifer Jones, Tracy Glover, Darla Davis, Towanan Wilson, and Flofine Mallard.

On his black steed in his cowboy gear, Woody MacDonald leads the young baseball players as they march down Gardens Boulevard (later renamed MacArthur Boulevard) in the parade for opening day of Little League in 1965.

Palm Beach Gardens' first recreation director, Woody Dukes, proudly presents the first piece of playground equipment. It was located at Plant Drive Park when it opened in 1965. What the park lacked in equipment was made up in parental enthusiasm.

86

After competing and finishing as a runner-up several times, the Palm Beach Gardens Parks and Recreation Department brought home the gold in 1989, becoming the National Gold Medal Winner in Recreation. The award-winning staff accepting the award includes, from left to right, (seated) Linda Bullock, recreation director Doug Hood, and Sue Ruskay Miller; (standing) Scott Moor, Bob Clarey, Lisa Polk, Christy Williams Murphy, Steve Cardorini, and Mike Fallon.

The Gardens' cheerleading team took first place in the World International Cheerleading Competition in Chicago in 1982, outperforming teams from the United States, Canada, and Great Britain. The team includes, from left to right, (kneeling) Chris Turley, Sarah McCarthy, Frankie Boyd, Cindy Vowell, Cathy Giroux, Julie Borders, Lesley Perez, and Chris Martin; (standing) Michael Martino, Greg McQuinn, Ben Woody, Richard Craney (captain), coach Suzanne Martin, Michelle Weaver (captain), Kenny Kepple, Mike Deskin, and Bert Premuroso.

John Keidis (far left) rides the sleigh with fellow council members, from left to right, Linda Monroe, Don Kiselewski, and Mike Martino aboard the City of Palm Beach Gardens float in the 1983 Christmas in Dixie Parade. The parade began in the parking lot at the Twin City Mall and continued south on US Highway 1 to Park Avenue, where it turned west, finishing at the railroad tracks.

Mayor Don Kiselewski rides in the rumble seat of an antique Ford in the 1982 Christmas in Dixie Parade. He was the grand marshal for the annual event sponsored by the Town of Lake Park. Palm Beach Gardens, North Palm Beach, Riviera Beach, and Lake Park were all represented in the parade, along with various civic and service groups, churches, dance schools, Boy Scouts, and Girl Scouts.

The Hetzel brothers prepare scenery for the Christmas Pageant displayed annually at MacArthur and Northlake Boulevards. In 1933, Conrad Hetzel was an invalid in Asheville, North Carolina. In a dream, he was told to create the pageant, and in doing so, he was cured. After moving to our area, the pageant was first staged at Curry Park and moved to the Gardens in the 1970s.

The Camp of the Magi was one of seven scenes of the Hetzel Christmas Pageant depicting the Christmas story. The scenes were constructed with thousands of scaled papier-mâché figures. When the pageant ended in the late 1980s, more than 80,000 people were attending the annual event. In addition to the Christmas pageant, an Easter pageant was also produced for a brief period.

Mayor Bob Diamond cuts the ribbon for the opening of Plant Drive Park on February 25, 1968. The park immediately became the hub of youth athletics and city events, with ball fields and basketball courts becoming the primary recreational magnets for the city's youth.

An accordion, saxophone, trumpet, drums, xylophone, and two washboards comprised this most unusual mixture of instruments, which made up the marching band for opening day ceremonies of the Little (Khoury) League baseball season in 1965. Here, the marchers parade in front of Howell Watkins Junior High, seen in the background.

Mayor Mike Martino and council members Don Kiselewski and Joe Russo were the marshals for the 1986 Macy's Day Parade at the opening of the Macy's store in The Gardens Mall.

Baseball Hall of Famer Gary Carter (left) prepares to board a float for the city's 1986 Spirit Parade with city council members, from left to right, Dick Feeney (with his granddaughter), Dick Aldred, Don Kiselewski, Mike Martino, and Linda Monroe. Each of these council members served as mayor at some point during his or her tenure.

Mayor Don Kiselewski and Leonard Devine, director of public works, pose with Miss Chief, the fire department's Dalmatian, prior to departing in the Spirit Parade. The parades were annual events in the late 1980s and moved from the city hall property to The Gardens Mall.

An early-1970s city tradition was a Christmas morning visit from Santa Claus (Leon Blanchard) on a fire truck. The siren sounded, and the children ran out to the street to get their treats. This was one of many events sponsored by the volunteer fire department.

Director of Parks and Recreation Doug Hood holds the city's 25th birthday commemorative plaque high before placing it in the "dented" casket that was donated to the city to use as a time capsule and buried in 1984. The last item thrown in the casket was an audiotape, which skipped as it played "The Star-Spangled Banner."

In 2005, Bill Kazakavage, a member of the public works crew who buried the time capsule 21 years earlier, reminded city officials of the capsule and its location. It was about to be covered by the construction of an addition to the recreation center, so council members David Levy (left), Mayor Joseph Russo (center), and Vice Mayor Eric Jablin opened the capsule. (Courtesy City of Palm Beach Gardens.)

The community chorus of North Palm Beach was founded in 1962. Beginning in Jupiter, it later changed its name to the North County Choral Society and then to the Choral Society of the Palm Beaches, Inc. The group is composed of volunteer singers who perform at three major concerts each year at the Borland Center Theatre, with encore performances at the Gardens Presbyterian Church.

The Morning Glories, a group of Palm Beach Gardens' women, have been bringing cheer to residents of nursing facilities throughout the county for more than 25 years. Since their inception, more than 100 women have participated, including, from left to right, (kneeling) Marilyn Glavin, Sally Schwartz, Sally Kaczor, Ann Shepard, Janie Berry, Pam Smith, and Gheratine Wilson; (standing) Kathy Hollenbeck, May Clark, Anna Fedorka, Sharon Wiley, Patti Penatta, and Fannie Assa.

Frank Chris (left) and Col. Dick Rule, members of the Exchange Club of the Northern Palm Beaches, pause to study the plan for mounting the 28 plaques depicting the documents that established the United States—the Freedom Shrine. Since this installation in 1977, numerous shrines have been installed in government buildings and schools in Palm Beach Gardens.

John Schneider (left), Bob DeYoung (center), and Don Kiselewski present a check for $12,000 to the Inter-City First Aid Ambulance Service from the Exchange Club of the Northern Palm Beaches in 1978. Inter-City was the only ambulance service serving the communities of the Northern Palm Beaches. The funds purchased telemetry equipment for ambulances to communicate with the Gardens' hospital and receive emergency medical information on patient care while transporting them.

In March 2004, the Palm Beach Gardens Woman's Club honored local women with a "Salute to Women Veterans of World War II." The event was in conjunction with the Library of Congress Veterans History Project. Honorees are, from left to right, Phyllis Grussing, Rozella Wood, Bernice Haydu, Kathleen Dedick, Jane Karrh, Betty Hill, Hazel Bundy, Helen Butterworth, Peggy Flynn, and Jo LeGault.

A traditional bagpiper leads the entrance parade for the dedication of the Veterans Plaza on November 11, 2007. It is located in front of city hall, on the east side. A dedication plaque with an Abraham Lincoln's quotation from 1863 sets the tone for the plaza: "Honor to the Soldier, and Sailor everywhere, who bravely bears his country's cause."

Mayor Don Kiselewski (left) presents a proclamation from the City of Palm Beach Gardens to, from left to right, John Chiodo, Fred Simcich, and James McCabe, congratulating them on the 100th birthday of the Knights of Columbus in 1982. Thomas V. Daily was the supreme chaplain of the Knights and Bishop of the Palm Beaches.

On October 21, 2011, the Seminole Chapter of the Daughters of the American Revolution (DAR) dedicated a historical marker at the city's entrance. It records the story of the city's beginnings in 1959 and the efforts of its founder, John D. MacArthur, in relocating banyan trees, the symbols of the city, to the entrance. State and Seminole Chapter Members of the DAR attending include, from left to right, Dawn Lemongello, Sue Comerford, Nicki Sabino, Betty Sither, Zee Porter, Phyllis Kelly, and Mary Alice Pugh.

Bicycles were the mode of travel for the youth of the Gardens in the 1970s, and bicycle safety was an important part of their training. Judy Hood points out the course to ride during the annual Bicycle Rodeo sponsored by the Palm Beach Gardens Woman's Club.

In 1974, neighbor kids rode together from the PGA Estates and the plat six area down the north side of Holly Drive, which was closed off to car traffic, allowing only bikes during school hours. Shown here are, from left to right, Chris Kiselewski, Holly Heath, Beth Truesdale, Heather Heath, Beverly Kiselewski, Sandy Sleeter, and Don Kiselewski Jr.

"The House that Buz Built" was completed in seven hours and 32 minutes on May 1, 1981, under the direction of Buz DiVosta. It set a record for minimum construction time and was placed in the Guinness Book of World Records. The home was built from scratch on a raw piece of ground, starting by forming the foundation, placing the concrete, framing the structure to the capping off, making it completely finished—inside and out—and even landscaped. The materials and the labor of over 500 workers were donated to the effort by local tradesmen. This was a true "barn raising" effort to get a swimming pool for the city, as the house was auctioned on May 11 for $155,000, with the proceeds being utilized to build city pool. Below, around 1982, lifeguard Don Kiselewski Jr. barks out safety instructions from his megaphone at the new pool.

City councils that play together stay together. Such was the case for these councilmen, from left to right, Don Kiselewski, Dick Aldred (back to camera), Joe Russo, and Mike Martino. They are participating in a sand sculpture competition between various city leaders in the area and sculpting a shapely lady sunning herself on the beach. They went on to capture first place at the first ArtiGras in 1985, which was held in Palm Beach Gardens.

From left to right, Jami Dolan, Jim Shiver, Tom Dolan, and Jeffery Masternich are starring in *No Sex Please, We're British*, one of many plays and musicals produced by local thespians. In 1979, the group organized in Lake Park, calling themselves the MacArthur Players and performing in the old Mirror Ballroom in the town hall before moving to the Gardens High School in 1980. That year, they changed their name to the Spotlite Players. Three years later, they relocated to the community center before disbanding in 1996.

In 1981, Jack Osborn, president and founder of the US Croquet Association, persuaded the PGA Sheraton Resort to add croquet courts to its premier sports complex. In 1987, five courts were dedicated, making the facility the largest croquet complex in the western hemisphere. He also convinced the USCA to move its headquarters from New York to Palm Beach Gardens. John Solomon is shown here at the 1988 US/International Invitational Cup.

In 1982, the Women's Tennis Association was headquartered in Palm Beach Gardens at PGA National Resort. Top professionals like Chris Evert (pictured) graced the courts for events like the Citizens Cup and Virginia Slims tournaments. Eight years later, in 1990, the headquarters moved, but the PGA Tennis Club remains a world-class facility.

Cub Scout Pack 176, here participating in the Christmas in Dixie Parade in 1976, was chartered at St. Ignatius Catholic Church in that same bicentennial year. The pack chartered with four dens and more than 30 boys. Don Kiselewski was the first cubmaster.

Girl Scouts Chris Kiselewski (left), Beth Truesdale (center), and Beverly Kiselewski proudly display their uniforms and posters of the badges that they have earned around 1975.

Ronnie Helsby gives a thumbs-up before taking off for a flight in an F-16 fighter. She organized the numerous military air and parachute shows in the early 1980s in Palm Beach Gardens.

Mayor Don Kiselewski and Congressman Tom Lewis discuss the progress of the "Missing Link" taskforce, whose mission was to expedite the completion of the 44-mile section of Interstate 95 between the Gardens and Fort Pierce. From the design of the link to the ribbon-cutting, it was pushed hard. The task force's efforts bore fruit when, in 1987, the "Missing Link" opened to traffic, 15 years ahead of its 2002 scheduled completion.

During the last nine years of his 12-year city council term, Don Kiselewski also chaired the Solid Waste Authority and the Metropolitan Planning Organization. To address the pressing garbage and trash situation, a $320 million Resource Recovery Plant facility was conceived, designed, financed, and constructed, and operations were begun. During this period, Kiselewski worked along with his counterparts in Broward and Dade Counties to establish and operate the Tri-Rail transportation system through the three counties.

In 1982, two 100-year storms occurred within several weeks of each other. The first storm dropped 23 inches of rain in 24 hours and turned Holly Drive into what residents called "Lake Holly."

Seven

THE GOLF CAPITAL
OF THE WORLD

"The Golf Capital of the World" is how John D. MacArthur referred to his new city. Always the astute businessman and far-sighted developer, he understood the value that an association with the game of golf would have in promoting the sale of residential property in South Florida.

While MacArthur was envisioning his dream city, The PGA of America, having outgrown its facilities in Dunedin, Florida, was looking around the state for property to build new headquarters. Chicago friends and PGA professionals Harry Pezzullo and Lou Strong, along with MacArthur's business advisor Jerry "Irish" Kelly, met and whittled out an agreement to create a first-class golf course development that would be a centerpiece for the proposed city and the new home of The Professional Golfers' Association (PGA) of America.

MacArthur took personal pride in the development of the golf course and clubhouse. Not only did he invest money to complete the project, he was also personally involved in every detail of the construction to make sure he achieved his objective. He hired prominent golf course architects Dick Wilson and Joe Lee to build the East and West Courses. A year later, the desolate land of sand, scrub, and palmetto trees was transformed into two spectacular courses that would rank among the top layouts in the country for years to come.

Even though the relationship between MacArthur and The PGA of America dissolved within 10 years, their dream of a city for golfers has become a reality and an unparalleled haven for those who love the game. Over the years, the city has hosted a number of professional golf tournaments and remains the permanent home of The PGA of America. Its membership has grown from 5,300 members in 1965 to more than 27,000 in 2012, with more than 100 of the members living in Palm Beach Gardens.

What began with a vision of a single premier golf community in the heart of the city continues 50 years later with nine golf communities and clubs that make up 17 courses of golfing enjoyment.

John D. MacArthur stands with a sign indicating his intention to make golf a catalyst for turning scrubland into prime residential property. Curiously, MacArthur knew very little about golf and did not play the game. However, he recognized a good business opportunity when it was presented to him. He was known to be extremely frugal, yet he spared no expense when it came to creating his premier golf facility.

The city's first golf community, developed by John D. MacArthur, was known as PGA National Golf Club from 1964–1973. The clubhouse with its distinctive turquoise tile roof was designed by renowned Miami architect Alfred Browning Parker. Known as a conservationist and environmentalist, Parker created buildings in a tropical Modernist style strongly influenced by Frank Lloyd Wright.

PGA professional Harry Pezzullo invited many of his celebrity friends—such as Perry Como, Bob Hope, and Jackie Gleason—to play at the club. They swapped golf stories around this memorable clubhouse bar, which was decorated with turquoise leather-covered barstools and photographs of golf professionals and celebrities who were guests at the club. Pezzullo was an integral part of the club from its inception until his death in 2005.

Of the 26 Senior PGA Championships held here between 1964 and 2000, Sam Snead holds the record, with six victories at PGA National Golf Club—in 1964, 1965, 1967, 1970, 1972, and 1973. His remarkable run was capped in 1973 by a 15-stroke victory. Snead (left) is pictured here receiving the trophy in 1965 from Ronald Teacher. (Photograph copyright The PGA of America. All rights reserved.)

The 53rd PGA Championship was held on the East Course February 25–29, 1971. Jack Nicklaus (pictured) won the Wanamaker Trophy, receiving the winning purse of $40,000 and becoming the first professional to win the Grand Slam twice. The hometown favorite, he shot rounds of 69–69–70–73=281, to beat Billy Casper by two strokes. (Photograph copyright The PGA of America. All rights reserved.)

The year 1971 was a banner year for golf at PGA National Golf Club and for Jack Nicklaus, who teamed with Lee Trevino to win the World Cup for the United States. John D. MacArthur (left) and Fred Corcoran, tournament director, are pictured here with Nicklaus, who also won in the individual category. Earlier in the year, Julius Boros won the Senior PGA Championship on the East Course with a total score of 285.

In 1973, MacArthur dissolved his agreement with The PGA of America and renamed his club JDM Country Club. This view looks across the 18th hole of the East Course towards the spacious open patio at the back of the clubhouse. For the next 15 years, JDM operated as a prestigious local golf and country club and continued to host many celebrities and professional golfers on its three famous golf courses. The PGA of America moved to temporary facilities in Lake Park and continued its search for a permanent home.

In 1988, the Hanson Group purchased the JDM Country Club. From its vision of a lush island paradise, it developed the private gated community that is known as BallenIsles Country Club. This is a picture of the redesigned 18th hole on the East Course. The club offers three golf courses—the acclaimed East, as well as the West and the South. (Courtesy BallenIsles.)

Under MacArthur's control, JDM Country Club was strictly a golf club. The Hanson Group demolished the old clubhouse and built a magnificent 72,000-square-foot clubhouse for golf and fine dining. BallenIsles is a five-star Platinum Club of America. In 2009, a 62,000-square-foot sports complex was completed. It included a Grand Slam Tennis and Fitness facility, pool, and 23 tennis courts with a viewing stadium. (Courtesy BallenIsles.)

The City of Palm Beach Gardens, in recognition of his win in the 53rd PGA Championship and the benefit of the PGA to the city, presented Jack Nicklaus with a key to the city on March 15, 1971. Pictured here, from left to right, are Councilman Tom Prentiss, City Manager Robert Carlson, Councilman John Orr, Jack Nicklaus, Mayor James DeLonga, Vice Mayor Walt Wiley, and Councilman Craig James.

Frank Cardi, president of The PGA of America; E. Llwyd Ecclestone Jr., president of National Investment Company; and Samuel Laurie, mayor, cut the ribbon to officially open PGA National Resort Community on March 2, 1980. Note the original PGA National logo on the wall in the background. (Courtesy *PGA National News*, Spring 1980.)

After 63 years of searching for a permanent home, The PGA of America built its headquarters in the PGA National Resort Community on land donated by E. Llwyd Ecclestone Jr. that he had purchased from John D. MacArthur. The headquarters opened in 1981, and from this location the PGA staff services the educational, tournament, financial, events, and administrative needs of PGA professionals throughout the United States. The PGA of America is the world's largest sports organization.

Shown here is the PGA National Resort Hotel, originally managed by the Sheraton Corporation. The golf shop is located in the west wing. In addition to four on-site and one off-site championship golf courses are the Members Clubhouse, Health and Racquet Club, croquet club, and a European spa known for its luxurious "Waters of the World."

The Honda Classic was founded in 1972 as Jackie Gleason's Inverrary Classic. Since 2007, the tournament has been played at PGA National Resort. Pictured above is Ernie Els, the 2008 champion. The Honda Classic is a PGA Tour event benefiting the Children's Healthcare Charity and the Nicklaus Children's Health Care Foundation. (Courtesy Children's Healthcare Charity.)

On March 4, 1980, E. Llwyd Ecclestone Jr., the developer of PGA National Resort Community, proudly opened the first of the four golf courses for play in his new community. "The Haig" was named for golfing great Walter Hagen, a major figure in golf in the first half of the 20th century. Hagan earned a total of 45 wins in his career. "The Champion," dedicated to all golf professionals, opened on November 17, 1981. It was the home for the Senior PGA Championship from 1982–2000, as well as the 1987 PGA Championship and the 1983 Ryder Cup. The course was redesigned by Jack Nicklaus in 2000 in preparation for the Honda Classic. The 15th, 16th, and 17th holes combine to create his famous "Bear Trap." "The Squire" is named in honor of Gene Sarazen, the first golfer ever to win the professional Grand Slam. It opened on October 30, 1981. The original three courses were designed by Tom and George Fazio. "The General," named for golf legend and course designer Arnold Palmer, was the last of the original four courses built, opening on February 28, 1984.

"The Champion" was the site of the 1983 Ryder Cup. Pictured in the middle is Jack Nicklaus, the United States captain, with the rest of the American team. Tony Jacklin was captain of the European team. The US team defeated Europe 14 1/2 to 13 1/2, with Lanny Wadkins's wedge shot on the last hole securing the win for the United States. (Courtesy PGA National Resort.)

The 69th PGA Championship was held August 6–9, 1987, at the PGA National Resort & Spa in Palm Beach Gardens, Florida. Larry Nelson won his second PGA Championship and third major title on the first sudden-death playoff hole over Lanny Wadkins. The victory produced the highest 72-hole score in PGA Championship history (287). (Courtesy PGA National Resort.)

Frenchman's Creek Beach and Country Club offers two demanding golf courses, the exclusive Beach Club on the ocean, and a private marina. In 1977, developers Burt Haft and Jack Gaines purchased the 1,400 acres of land, formerly owned by the Hoyts, from the John D. and Catherine T. MacArthur Foundation. Part of this property included two public golf courses, which became Frenchman's Creek Country Club. (Courtesy www.frenchmanscreek.com.)

Designed by George Fazio, the 7,011-yard, par-72 course at Eastpointe Country Club opened in 1974. In 1972, Eastpointe Towers Condominium was built on Singer Island at the easternmost point of Florida. While marketing their condominiums, the developers decided to find land to build a golf and tennis facility for the apartment buyers, creating Eastpointe Country Club in the process. (Courtesy Eastpointe Country Club.)

Old Marsh Golf Club was built in 1987. The 16th hole, seen here, is a 176-yard par 3. Providing a rare glimpse of Old Florida, the 7,021-yard, 18-hole layout winds through 456 acres of marsh sanctuary. The course was carefully crafted by renowned golf course designer Pete Dye to blend harmoniously with the native ecosystem. Majestic pines, saw grass vistas, and pristine oak hammocks remain virtually undisturbed. (Courtesy Old Marsh.)

The Palm Beach Gardens Municipal Golf Course opened in 1992. This par-72, Roy Case–designed course is one of the only golf courses in Florida to wind through natural preserve and wetlands areas. Pictured here at the ground-breaking are, from left to right, Councilmen Don Kiselewski and Joe Russo, Mayor Mike Martino, and City Manager John Orr.

Frenchman's Reserve is an Arnold Palmer Signature golf course community built in 2002. Played from the gold tees, the par-72 course is 6,867 yards of challenging golf. The community offers 447 customized homes in the architectural style of 20th-century architect Addison Mizner as well as an array of social and sporting activities. (Courtesy Frenchman's Reserve.)

Built in 2001, Mirasol Country Club is a magnificent 2,300-acre community surrounded by natural preserves and exquisite lakes. The private, gated enclave, located just west of the turnpike, offers two championship courses—"Sunrise" and "Sunset"—designed by legendary golf course architects Tom Fazio and Arthur Hills, plus a premier sports-and-fitness center with tennis, pool, and spa. (Courtesy Mirasol.)

The stunning gates at Old Palm Golf Club welcome just 330 members into the exclusive golf club community with custom estate residences. The limited membership at Old Palm allows a "no tee-time" policy on the Raymond Floyd–designed course. Members also enjoy the unique 33-acre Golf Learning Studio and clubhouse, which offers casual and formal dining, a fitness center, a full-service spa, a pool, and concierge services. (Courtesy Old Palm.)

"Mr. Mac," John D. MacArthur, seen here basking in the glory of his dream come true, is surrounded by some of golf's legendary players at the award-winning golf club that he built. To the right of John D. MacArthur (second from left) are golf professionals Gene Sarazen— wearing his traditional "plus four" pants—Sam Snead, and Skip Alexander. MacArthur is wearing his customary attire—a cardigan.

Eight

TODAY AND TOMORROW

June 2009 brought the 50th anniversary of Palm Beach Gardens. The city was founded to be a verdant paradise, and it is, with green spaces, golf courses, and parks coexisting with residential and commercial areas. Carefully placed works of "Art in Public Places" (AIPP) also animate the city. Since 1988, the city code has required developers with projects valued over $1 million to donate one percent of that value to AIPP. The developers select the artists and the sites and provide for future maintenance. A seven-member AIPP advisory board must approve, as must the city council.

Residents turned out en masse for the multifaceted 50th anniversary celebration on Saturday, November 21, 2009. Children's games, musical artists, multitudinous food offerings, historical displays, and a classic car show were the main activities. The culminating event was the presentation of a statue of the city's founder, John D. MacArthur, made possible by a grant from the John D. and Catherine T. MacArthur Foundation.

The future of Palm Beach Gardens is economically secure. In March 2011, aerospace firm Chromalloy, citing the city as a rich source of engineering talent, announced it as the new location of its corporate headquarters. In April, Florida Power & Light, a Fortune 500 company, purchased a prime 80-acre tract here for "expansion options." To support the city's role in the north county's biotech hub, city council members promoted an increase of biotechnology courses at Palm Beach State College. In addition, they cooperated in the 2009 opening of the Scripps Research Institute at Florida Atlantic University in neighboring Jupiter and pledged PBG-owned land adjacent to the campus for phase-two development. Further, they welcomed the Max Planck Florida Institute, which, in collaboration with Scripps, ensures a knowledge-based economy that will supply high-salaried jobs and pay enormous medical, educational, and social dividends to Palm Beach Gardens.

Double Rainbows by sculptor Lila Katzen was the first Art in Public Places (AIPP) installation. In the early 1980s, the sculpture was placed on the south side of Palm Beach Gardens City Hall; but in 1989, because of the construction of the current city hall, it was moved to the grounds of the Burns Road Community Center.

Contiguous Currents by Greek-born artist Costas Varotsos is located in the municipal complex along North Military Trail. The turquoise sculpture is a twisting line of curved metal with lower sections suggestive of pools of water. Despite the artist's worldwide reputation, this untraditional sculpture is arguably the city's most controversial artwork. While some residents appreciate it, others call it "the wave," which is not a compliment, or worse—"snakes."

Each of the four towers atop the PGA Boulevard flyover bridge houses an elegant steel mesh sculpture by Maryland artist Wendy Ross. Each suspended metal sphere is about five feet in diameter. Below each sphere is transparent steel mesh fabricated to resemble a sea fan. Sunlight reflects off this mesh during the day, and colored lights give it brilliance at night. The artist envisioned her creation as "a visual tapestry of motion, light, and steel," and the result is a delight to the mind and the eye. The work was dedicated in November 2006. Below, the unusual sculptures can be seen within the four towers, two on each side of the overpass left of the Florida East Coast Railway tracks, just west of The Gardens Mall.

9-11-01, made with scorched metal beams from the World Trade Center, was dedicated by Mayor David Levy, Police Chief Stephen Stepp, and Fire Chief Peter Bergel in a somber ceremony on September 11, 2010. The 36-foot girders were chosen by sculptor Mark Fuller in New York City. Palm Beach Gardens firemen and policemen escorted the flag-draped beams to the city in a motorcycle brigade.

At the 50th anniversary celebration of Palm Beach Gardens on Saturday, November 21, 2009, the Five Boroughs and their backup band provided live music and entertainment. The party, held at the Burns Road Community Center, lasted from 4:00 p.m. until 9:00 p.m., and approximately 5,000 residents attended.

Amara Shriners Komic Klowns entertain children and adults alike. There was great child participation in the celebration. An entire section left of the community center was devoted to children's games, including ring and ball toss, chalk sidewalk drawing, races, miniature golf, a treasure hunt, and "fishing." Several crafts were also enjoyed, and the creations of pipe cleaners and beads were popular.

Some residents examine the classic car exhibit in the front parking lot along Burns Road as busy booths sell food, crafts, 50th-anniversary memorabilia, and other merchandise in the background. The first 3,000 attendees were offered free hot dogs, chips, and drinks.

After the presentation of the larger-than-life MacArthur statue, seen in the background, past and present city council members gather together. From left to right, they are David Levy, Eugene Walker, Bert Premuroso, Don Kiselewski, Jody Barnett, Harold Valeche, George Bonner, Eric Jablin, Michael Martino, Joseph Russo, Annie Marie Delgado, and Walter Wiley.

The Palm Beach Community College (PBCC) bioscience building was dedicated on May 28, 2008, by, from left to right, PBCC trustee Carolyn Williams; Dr. Patricia Anderson, North Campus provost; Dr. Dennis Gallon, PBCC president; and Mayor Joseph Russo. The college, now Palm Beach State College, will use this state-of-the-art facility to strengthen partnerships with various biotech institutes in the area, as well as nearby Florida Atlantic University (FAU).

Standing beside Dr. Richard A. Lerner, president of the Scripps Research Institute, Florida governor Charles Crist (right) cuts the ribbon on February 26, 2009, to open the biomedical facility on FAU's John D. MacArthur Campus. Palm Beach Gardens will enable an expanded north county biotech hub by providing an educated workforce and the necessary land. (Photograph by James McEntee, courtesy Scripps Research Institute.)

On April 7, 2011, the CEO and scientific director of the Max Planck Florida Institute, Dr. David Fitzpatrick (standing behind the company logo), prepares to sign the central beam in the topping-off ceremony for the new facility at FAU, scheduled to open in spring 2012. Operating in temporary FAU quarters since 2009, the institute adds a strong international component to the county's life sciences cluster. (Courtesy the O'Donnell Agency.)

The eight-foot statue of John D. MacArthur, sculpted by Pennsylvania artist Zenos Frudakis, was installed, after some debate over its location, within the municipal complex on North Military Trail. Here in the center of Palm Beach Gardens, MacArthur can watch over and marvel at what his city has and will become. Of course, he originally conceived of Palm Beach Gardens to make money. However, as he revealed to his friend Stewart Alsop, who was interviewing him for an article entitled "America's New Big Rich," "You see something coming out of the ground. You see houses and bicycles and kids, where there was nothing but palmettos and rattlesnakes—that gives you more of a thrill than anything else."

John D. MacArthur
Founder of the City of Palm Beach Gardens

Bronze

Commissioned by
City of Palm Beach Gardens

Support provided by
John D. and Catherine T. MacArthur Foundation

Zenos Frudakis, sculptor, 2009

ABOUT THE
ORGANIZATION

The seven authors of this book are, from left to right, Don Kiselewski, Arline Kiselewski, Suzy Bryant, Linda Smith, Maria Mamlouk, Irene Pedrick, and Walt Wiley. They are standing outside the home of the Palm Beach Gardens Historical Society at 5312 Northlake Boulevard on the south campus of Christ Fellowship.

Founded in 2008, the society is a nonprofit, nongovernmental, volunteer organization whose mission is to collect, preserve, and share the rich history of the city for the education and enjoyment of current and future generations.

To that end, the society sponsors monthly enrichment programs featuring noted speakers familiar with the Palm Beach Gardens area. Social events are also enjoyed, and the archiving of historical materials is ongoing.

The society welcomes new members. For further information, consult the website at www. pbghistoricalsociety.org.

Visit us at
arcadiapublishing.com

....